Outdoor Guides
FIRST AID &
EMERGENCIES

Lauris Morgan-Griffiths

Illustrated by Malcolm English
and Jonathan Langley
Designed by Sally Burrough
Edited by Rosamund Kidman Cox
and Bridget Gibbs

Additional artwork by
Andy Martin
and Sally Burrough

Design Assistant
Niki Overy

Acknowledgements
We would like to thank the
following organizations for their
help in producing this book:

The staff of the St. John
Ambulance Association in Britain
and Australia
The staff of the Royal Life Saving
Society
The staff of the London
Fire Brigade

We would also like to thank
Beatrice Tannant
SRN, RSCN, SCM, RN Canada,
for her assistance.

First published in 1979 by Usborne Publishing
Ltd., 20 Garrick Street, London WC2E 9BJ,
England.

Copyright © 1979 Usborne Publishing Ltd.

Published in Canada by Hayes Publishing Ltd.,
Burlington, Ontario.

Printed in Great Britain

Contents

4 First Aid
6 Getting help
8 Breathing
10 Consciousness
12 Shock
14 Burns
16 Bleeding
18 Bandages
20 Using a roller bandage
22 Using a triangular bandage
24 Fractures and sprains
26 General injuries and ailments
32 Signalling for help
34 Ground-to-air signals
36 Heat hazards
38 Cold hazards
40 Fires in forest and grassland
42 Natural disasters
46 Danger on water
48 Saving others from water
50 Saving yourself from water
53 Points to remember
54 Poisonous plants
56 Animals that sting
58 Poisonous animals
60 Dangerous animals
62 Book list/Useful addresses
63 Index

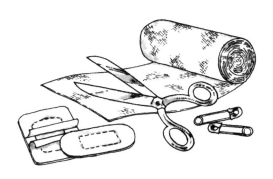

First Aid

Outdoor activities such as walking and camping are fun, but one day you, or one of your friends, may have an accident. Accidents always happen unexpectedly, so it is vital that you know what to do immediately.

The first half of the book tells you what to do in a serious emergency and how to treat general injuries and ailments. Practise some of the bandaging in your spare time and learn how to put someone into the recovery position.

The second half shows you how to deal with dangerous situations that might occur on land and water and tells you about poisonous and dangerous plants and animals.

Assembling an emergency kit

Whenever you go walking, cycling or boating, take an emergency kit with you. Although you probably won't need it, you should always carry it with you just in case. Check the kit before you go out, and replace any items as they are used. Keep it simple; if it is too bulky it will be too heavy to carry very far. Most of the things needed can be bought cheaply or found around the house. Keep them in plastic bags or in a seal-top plastic box.

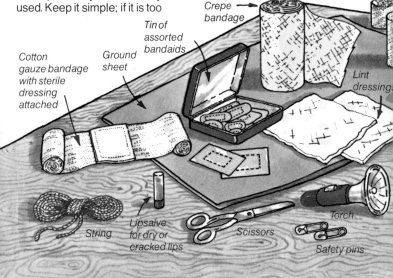

Crepe bandage

Tin of assorted bandaids

Cotton gauze bandage with sterile dressing attached

Ground sheet

Lint dressing

String

Lipsalve for dry or cracked lips

Scissors

Torch

Safety pins

What is first aid?

First Aid is acting fast and doing all you can to help an injured person before professional help arrives. In a serious accident, your actions could even mean the difference between life and death. Even minor injuries should be treated carefully; if they are not attended to promptly they may become worse.

In any accident there are four things you must do before you attend to anything else:
1. Make sure that you are not in any danger yourself; it is much better to go and get help rather than put yourself in a situation where your own life may be at risk.
2. Check that the person is breathing; make sure that the airways are clear (page 9).
3. Stop any serious bleeding (pages 16/17).
4. Check that the person is conscious (pages 10/11).
ONLY when you have checked these things should you begin to worry about any other injuries. The order is easy to remember:
ABC
A = Airways
B = Bleeding
C = Consciousness
There is one other important thing to remember – the injured person will be upset and frightened. Reassure him and don't leave him alone. If help is needed, send someone else to organize it.

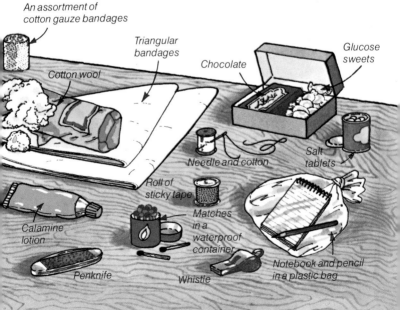

An assortment of cotton gauze bandages

Triangular bandages

Chocolate

Glucose sweets

Cotton wool

Needle and cotton

Salt tablets

Roll of sticky tape

Calamine lotion

Matches in a waterproof container

Notebook and pencil in a plastic bag

Penknife

Whistle

5

Getting help

Apply ABC emergency first aid *before* you go for help (page 5). *Never* leave an unconscious person alone. If someone is in need of urgent medical help – i.e. he is in danger of death, has severe injuries, or is in bad pain, send someone to find a telephone to call the emergency services. If he has minor injuries, call the local doctor. (If the number is not in the telephone directory, ask the operator.) In bad weather, don't let anyone go for help alone; wait until conditions improve.

If there is no-one else with you and the accident is really so serious that you must leave the person to get help, make sure that he is still breathing and conscious, and that bleeding has not started again. Make the person warm and as comfortable as possible, and tell him how long you think you will be away. If you think you will be away for some time, leave a whistle so that he can signal for help. Make sure you can find your way back to the place where you left the person.

Making an emergency call

The emergency number will be displayed in the phone box (999 in Britain). The call is free. The operator will ask you for your exchange, phone number and the service you want (fire, police or ambulance).

Fire

Describe where the fire is. Give brief details of the type of fire – car, house or forest – and whether anyone is trapped.

Police

If you are worried about what service to ask for, ring the police. They will contact the other services. Tell them your name and where you are.

Ambulance

Describe clearly where you want them to go, explain what has happened, how many people are hurt and the type of injuries.

Carrying a person with minor injuries

Human crutch

Pick-a-back

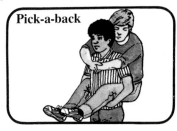

4-handed seat

If someone has a minor injury, help them to the nearest shelter or house. If the person is conscious and is capable of holding on to you, he could be carried by one of the methods shown here. Before moving anyone, check for serious injuries. If they are badly hurt don't move them in case you make the injury worse.

Road accidents

First make sure that you are not in any danger. Only move the casualty if he is in danger of being run over or the car is likely to explode. Get someone to warn approaching traffic and reduce any risk of fire by turning off the car engine; then attend to the casualty. Check that he is breathing (pages 8/9) and stop any heavy bleeding (pages 16/17). Deal with these three things first; minor injuries can be seen to later. Send for help and reassure the casualty. Listen to what he says about any pain, sickness or dizziness, which could indicate other injuries.

7

Breathing

To find out if someone is breathing, watch to see if his chest is rising and falling. If there are no signs of breathing, clear the mouth of any objects, blood, or vomit, so that the airways are clear. Tilt his head well back. If he does not begin to breathe, start artificial respiration.

Choking

Choking is caused by something blocking the airways. The person may or may not be coughing, but he will be red in the face. You must remove whatever is stuck in the throat before it stops him breathing. Thump him hard on the back several times to dislodge the object. Put a child head down over your knee, then thump him on the back. With a very young child, hold him up by the legs and slap him on the back. If, when you have removed the object, the person has stopped breathing (he will be white or blue in the face), start artificial respiration.

Suffocation

Suffocation is caused by something stopping air reaching the lungs. It may be an object (e.g. a plastic bag over the head) or smoke filling the airways. Remove anything over the face, or drag the person away from the danger. Start artificial respiration if breathing has stopped. If you are entering a smoke-filled room, first make sure you can get out. Go in on your hands and knees.

Artificial respiration

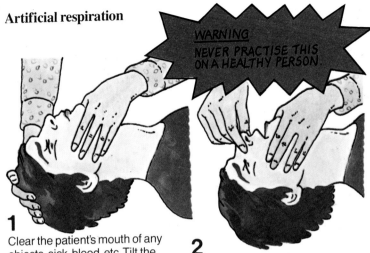

WARNING
NEVER PRACTISE THIS ON A HEALTHY PERSON.

1
Clear the patient's mouth of any objects, sick, blood, etc. Tilt the head back with the chin pushed forward. This straightens out the airways and the person may start breathing again. If he does, put him in the recovery position (page 11).

2
If the person is breathing only faintly, or not at all, keep his head tilted back, open his mouth with one hand and with your other hand pinch his nostrils firmly together.

3

Take a deep breath. Cover his mouth with your lips and blow deeply into his lungs. Repeat this quickly four times so that you fill his lungs with air. Remove your mouth and wait for his chest to fall. If he fails to breathe, start artificial respiration again.

4
If he is still failing to breathe, there may be something stuck in his windpipe. Turn the person onto his side and thump him hard between the shoulder blades. Turn him back again. Put his head to one side and remove anything that is in his mouth. Tilt his head back with the chin forward and start artificial respiration again.

If breathing still fails to start, turn him on his side again and thump between the shoulder blades, then turn him back and remove anything in the mouth. Continue artificial respiration. Repeat these actions until breathing actually starts or help arrives.

Consciousness

If a person is unconscious don't waste time attending to small injuries; concentrate on making him breathe properly. There are different degrees of consciousness (explained below). Watch how the person is behaving so you can tell if his condition is getting any worse. Be prepared – people are often sick before they lapse into, or as they come round from unconsciousness.

The four stages of consciousness

a. Fully conscious: awake and able to talk.
b. Drowsy: keeps falling asleep, but is easily woken.
c. Stupor: only woken when pain is inflicted – try pinching the person. He will not be able to give proper answers to questions.
d. Cannot be woken at all. Pupils are dilated.

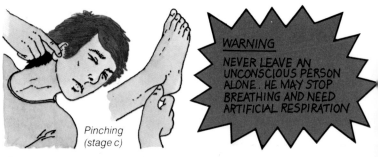

Pinching
(stage c)

WARNING

NEVER LEAVE AN UNCONSCIOUS PERSON ALONE. HE MAY STOP BREATHING AND NEED ARTIFICIAL RESPIRATION

How to treat an unconscious person

Clear the mouth of any loose objects. With a hanky wrapped round your finger, wipe away any vomit, blood or loose teeth.

Loosen any tight clothing round the neck, waist and chest. Turn him over gently into the recovery position (see opposite).

The recovery position

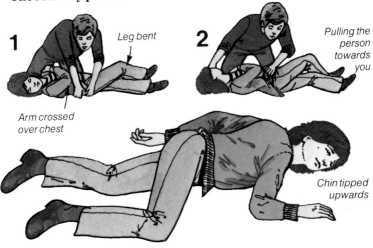

1 Leg bent

Arm crossed over chest

2 Pulling the person towards you

Chin tipped upwards

This is the best position for an unconscious person to lie in; the airways are clear so the person can breathe easily and will not choke. To put him in the recovery position, place the arm nearest you palm down underneath the body. Cross the other arm over the chest and bend the leg furthest from you over the other one (1). Support the head with your hand and roll the person over by pulling on the clothes around the hips (2). Keep the airways open by tipping the chin upwards to straighten the neck. There is now little danger of the person choking; even so, don't leave him on his own.

3 Make him comfortable. If possible put a coat underneath him and cover him with another. Don't put anything under his head. He needs lots of fresh air, so keep back any crowds that may gather.

4 Keep a close check on his breathing. If it stops, start artificial respiration at once (pages 8/9). If he starts to come round, reassure him by talking. Be prepared for him to be sick.

11

Shock

Some degree of shock occurs after most accidents. Watch the injured person for signs of shock, even if the injury is minor. The worse the injury, the worse the shock. A serious state of shock can be very dangerous.

Signs to look for

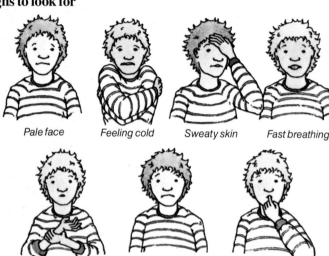

Pale face *Feeling cold* *Sweaty skin* *Fast breathing*

Rapid and weak pulse *Feeling sick* *Seeming anxious or vague*

How to take someone's pulse

Blood is moved around the body by a pumping action of the heart. At certain points of the body you can feel a pulse which tells you how regular the pumping action is. A rapid and weak pulse is a sign of shock; an irregular pulse signals a possible heart attack.

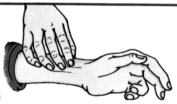

The easiest place to feel a pulse is on the wrist. Place your fingers just below the thumb joint on the wrist of your other hand. Move your fingers around until you find the pulse, then count the number of beats in 30 seconds. Multiply the number by two: this gives the

DO'S...		... & DON'TS
		**DON'T GIVE PATIENT A HOT WATER BOTTLE. THIS DRAWS BLOOD FROM HEART AND LUNGS TO THE SKIN. DO KEEP HIM WARM**
		DON'T GIVE DRINKS
LIE PATIENT DOWN WITH LEGS RAISED. (UNLESS THEY ARE BROKEN)	LOOSEN CLOTHING AT NECK, CHEST AND WAIST TO MAKE PATIENT COMFY	**DON'T MOVE PERSON UNNECESSARILY, ESPECIALLY IF INJURIES ARE BAD**

RAISE SHOULDERS AND TURN HEAD TO ONE SIDE. IF HEAD, CHEST OR ABDOMEN IS INJURED	IF PATIENT IS SICK OR UNCONSCIOUS, PLACE IN RECOVERY POSITION

COVER WITH SHEET OR BLANKET TO PROTECT FROM COLD	IF PATIENT IS THIRSTY, WET LIPS WITH WATER	**REMEMBER** **DON'T HESITATE TO CALL AN AMBULANCE IF THE SHOCK OR INJURY IS SERIOUS**

rate per minute.

Take your pulse again after some exercise and it will almost certainly be higher. The average adult pulse rate when resting is 60-80 beats per minute. The rate is higher in children: between 90 and 100 beats a minute. The rate varies from person to person. The main reason for taking a pulse is to see that it is regular and strong. The neck pulse can sometimes be easier to find, so try taking the pulse at the neck, as shown here.

Burns

Burns can be caused by contact with fire, hot objects, electricity, hot fat, boiling water, steam or dangerous chemicals. A burn causes loss of the liquid part of the blood, called plasma, from the tissues. The plasma either collects under the skin, forming blisters, or it leaks away if the skin is broken. The amount of plasma lost over a large area can be very serious. Never apply ointment. Only very minor burns should be bandaged. Concentrate on taking the heat out of the burn and then send for help. Treat for shock (pages 12/13).

Cool the burnt area

Apply cold water immediately to the burnt area. The faster you act, the less damage will be done. Use slow running water – a tap, hose or a running stream. If no running water is available, use a bucket of water but, if possible, avoid stagnant pond water. Leave the burn submerged for at least ten minutes. Running water should also remove any chemicals still sticking to the flesh.

If electricity has been involved, first make sure that the current has been switched off and is not still passing through the person's body (page 28); if he has stopped breathing, start artificial respiration (page 9).

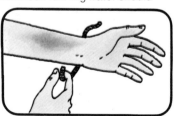

Take off anything tight, such as a watch or a shoe, before the area begins to swell.

Removing clothing

Don't remove charred clothing unless it is smouldering; it will have been sterilized by the burning. **Never remove any clothing stuck to a burn.** Though water should wash away any chemicals, do remove clothes that have been soaked by a chemical; be careful not to get chemicals on your hands.

Minor burns

First cool the injury for at least ten minutes under slow running water. Then, if the skin is unbroken, the affected area appears to be small, and, after half an hour, there is no blistering, treat it as a minor burn. If the area is still wet, gently dry it with cotton wool. Apply a sterile dressing and gently bandage (page 20).

Major burns

Wet cloth

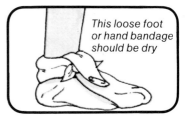

This loose foot or hand bandage should be dry

If the area has blistered or the skin is broken and weeping, this is a serious burn. Send for an ambulance. If possible, put the blistered area under slow running water and then cover with a cloth. If the burn covers a large area, you may not be able to place it under running water and it might be unwise to move the patient. In this case, gently cover the area with a wet cloth; keep wetting the cloth with cold water as it warms up. Get the person to lie down. If the burn is on a foot or hand you can gently tie a dry cloth into a bandage after the area has been cooled (page 23 and above).

If the burn is on a limb, raise the limb and support it in a comfortable position to stop swelling. The person will probably be suffering from shock (pages 12/13), so loosen clothing round the neck, chest and waist and keep the person warm. If he is conscious, give him regular sips of cold water to replace the loss of plasma "water" from the wound. Give reassurance and watch for signs of severe shock.

Bleeding

Serious bleeding must be stopped immediately by applying pressure to the cut or wound with a roller bandage, a pressure pad, or the fingers. Don't apply a torniquet – it may cut off the blood supply completely and result in permanent damage. Send or go for help after you have applied first aid. The person may have lost a lot of blood, and this must be replaced by a blood transfusion in hospital.

What to do

If the wound is a clean cut, you can apply pressure by holding the cut edges together. If the bleeding is from a large area, use a dressing as a pressure pad, pressing it firmly over the area.

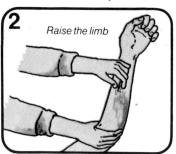

Raise the limb

If the injury is on a limb and there are no broken bones, hold the limb up so the blood flows away from the wound. Continue to apply pressure for at least ten minutes, even on a finger cut.

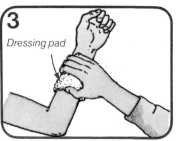

Dressing pad

If you have been holding the cut, apply a dressing (use material if no dressings are available). If there is glass or metal in the wound, put a ring pad over the dressing (page 19), then bandage.

Gauze bandage

If bleeding is very bad, place another dressing over the first one to give more pressure. Bandage firmly with a roller bandage in the figure of eight manner (pages 20 21).

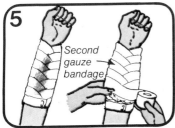

5

Second gauze bandage

Don't be tempted to remove the bandage to look at the wound. You might restart the bleeding. If blood seeps through, add more pads and another bandage over the first one.

6

If the person appears to be suffering from shock (pages 12/13), get her to lie down and keep her warm. Raise her legs and rest them on a stone or rucksack so more blood goes to the head.

7

If much blood has been lost, the person will lose consciousness; put them into the recovery position (page 11). Send for help, but don't leave the unconscious person alone.

Internal bleeding

Each person has, on average, about 6 litres (10 pints) of blood in his body. This circulates around the body in tubes or blood vessels called veins, arteries and capillaries.

A severe blow to the body may break blood vessels under the skin so blood leaks inside the body. Bruising is in fact bleeding under the skin.

Internal bleeding may not show on the skin as bruising if the injury is inside the body. If, after an accident, a person looks pale and ill, their skin feels cold (especially the hands and feet), and the pulse rate rises, they may be suffering from bad internal bleeding.

Other signs are a large swelling, very bad pain and/or severe shock. A lot of blood can be lost internally around broken bones: as much as two pints can be lost around a broken thigh bone.

The only first aid you can give to someone with internal bleeding is to raise the swollen limb *(unless it is broken)* and make the person rest. Treat them for shock (pages 12/13) and send or go for help.

Bandages

Bandages are used to hold a dressing in place, to put pressure on a wound so as to stop bleeding, or to hold still an injured part of the body. If possible, a wound should be covered with a clean dressing before it is bandaged. The most common types of bandages are roller and triangular. If, in an emergency, you haven't got your first aid kit, you can make dressings or bandages out of scarves, clothes or hankies.

Roller bandages

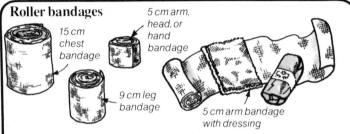

15 cm chest bandage

5 cm arm, head, or hand bandage

9 cm leg bandage

5 cm arm bandage with dressing

Roller bandages are made of elasticated crepe or cotton gauze. Crepe bandages are used when support is needed, for example when bandaging an injured joint. Cotton gauze roller bandages come in rolls of various widths for the different parts of the body; for example, finger bandages are 2.5 cm wide, leg bandages 9 cm wide, and chest bandages are 15 cm wide. You can buy gauze bandages with sterile dressings included in the packet. These bandages are also useful for putting pressure on badly bleeding cuts.

Triangular bandages

A triangular bandage is made of calico or linen, but in an emergency you can make one by cutting a one-metre square of material diagonally into two. This very useful all-purpose bandage can be made into a

Triangular calico bandage

sling or ring pad, or folded to make a narrow bandage which can be then used like a roller bandage (see opposite).

How to make a narrow bandage

Fold the point of the triangle over so it touches the base, then fold the bandage in half. This gives you a broad bandage, which could be used to hold a large dressing in place. The broad bandage folded in half makes a narrow bandage which can be used to hold a dressing in place or to immobilize a limb (page 25).

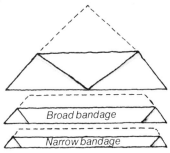

Broad bandage

Narrow bandage

How to make a ring pad

A wound over a possible fracture, or a wound containing grit or large splinters should be covered with a loose dressing. A ring pad placed on top will keep pressure off the wound when the bandage is applied.

With the end of a narrow bandage make a double loop around your hand. Take the loop off your hand and wind the bandage round it. Continue winding until you have made a firm ring. Tuck in the end. The ring pad should be large enough to encircle the wound.

Fastening bandages

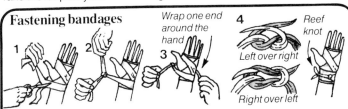

Wrap one end around the hand

Reef knot

Left over right

Right over left

Bandages can be fastened with sticky tape or safety pins, or they can be tie-fastened. When using a safety pin, double the bandage end over to make a neat edge and then pin.

When tying a knot, cut the end of the bandage lengthwise into two (1). Knot these two ends to stop the bandage splitting (2). Then wrap one of the ends round the hand (3) and tie it to the other end (4). A reef knot is flat and tidy; it is easy to untie but it will not slip undone.

Using a roller bandage

Figure-of-eight roller bandaging is used to support an injured limb or joint. You also use this type of bandaging to hold a dressing in place over a cut.

Before bandaging, wash your hands. Cover an open wound with a dressing, being careful not to touch the wound or the underside of the dressing. If, however, the person is bleeding badly, don't worry about hygiene or correct bandaging – quickly wind a bandage firmly around the wound (see also pages 16/17).

Figure-of-eight roller bandaging

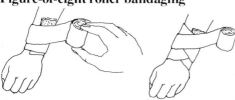

Face the person. Start by placing the bandage at an angle below the injury and on the dressing. Wind it firmly round twice to fix the dressing in place. Hold up the roll of bandage and, unrolling it a little at a time, start to wind it round the limb in a figure of eight. At each turn, overlap the previous wind of the bandage. Keep the bandaging at an even pressure. Finish above the injury with two firm turns on top of one another, then fasten.

Finger (cut, minor burn)

Fix the dressing in place with a couple of turns of the bandage (1). Criss-cross up the finger, away from the nail. Loop the bandage over the finger tip as shown (2).

Criss-cross down the finger (3) and then back up again, so that you cover the loop. Finish at the base of the finger (4) and tie with a reef knot (page 19).

Elbow or knee (cut)

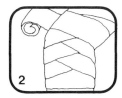
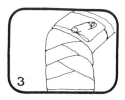

If possible, use an elasticated crepe bandage for an elbow or knee; it gives support while

allowing some movement of the joint. Hold the dressing in place with a couple of turns of

the bandage; then criss-cross around the joint. Finish above the injury. Fasten a crepe bandage with a safety pin.

Hand or wrist (cut)

For a hand wound, secure the dressing with a couple of turns of the bandage (1), then criss-cross up the hand (2). Take the bandage around the wrist to secure it; finish it here (3). For a wrist wound (4),

criss-cross around the wrist, then secure the bandage with a couple of loops around the hand. Finish with a couple of turns around the wrist.

Foot or ankle (cut)

For a foot wound, secure the dressing with a couple of turns (1), then criss-cross up the foot. Take the bandage around the ankle to secure it (2); finish here (3). For an ankle wound (4) criss-cross

around the ankle then secure the bandage with a couple of loops around the foot. Finish with a couple of turns around the ankle. If the shoe has to be kept on, just bandage around the ankle.

Using a triangular bandage

Ordinary sling

Use this type of sling to give support to an injured arm. The arm may also need to be supported if the ribs have been injured. Hold the forearm of the injured side steady while applying the bandage. Lay the bandage

over the body as shown; the hand should be slightly higher than the elbow. Raise the lower point of the bandage and tie it to the point on the shoulder. The sling should now take the weight of the arm. Fold the point at the elbow and pin it.

Make-do slings

Pin sleeve to jacket

Padding

Padding

Padding

Turn up lower edge of jacket and pin to collar

Use a belt, scarf, or tie

Padding

Sling (badly injured arm, shoulder or collar bone)

Lay the arm across the chest, with the palm down. The hand should be higher than the elbow; this is a comfortable position and may reduce any swelling. Lay the bandage over the arm as shown. Hold the arm steady and ease the base of the bandage under the hand, arm and elbow. Pass the lower end under the elbow and round the back to the uninjured shoulder. Tie the two ends in the hollow above the collar bone. Tuck the point in the crook of the elbow. Fold over the remaining material and pin.

Foot or hand (burn)

Put the foot (or hand) on the bandage and bring the point over the foot (or palm). Cross the two ends over the point and bring them around the back of the ankle (or wrist), then round to the front. Tie in front of the ankle (or on top of the wrist).

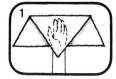

Turn point over knot and pin

1 Elbow or knee (burn)

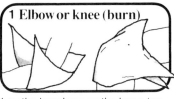

Lay the bandage on the knee (or under the elbow). Bring the two ends around behind the knee (over the elbow), cross them over, bring them round to the front and tie. (For an elbow, tie behind the arm.)

1 Scalp (cut)

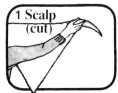

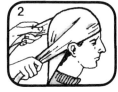

Pin point over knot

Turn over the long edge of the bandage to make a hem. Place this edge just above the eyebrows. Bring the ends down behind the head, keeping the ears uncovered. Cross the ends and tie in the middle of the forehead. Pin up the point.

Is the bandage too tight?

Bandages, especially roller bandages, must be applied firmly, but if they are too tight they can cut off blood circulation. Try taking the pulse. If you can't feel it, test to see if the bandage is too tight by pressing a finger-nail or toe-nail of the bandaged limb so that it turns white. The nail should turn pink again when the pressure is removed. If it stays white or blue, or if the fingers or toes are cold, numb or tingling, loosen the bandage slightly, but do not take it off.

Fractures and sprains

A fracture is a broken or a cracked bone. Without an X-ray it is difficult to tell a fracture from a sprain. Also, a sprain could have an underlying fracture, so treat a sprain as a fracture. Don't move someone with a fracture; you could cause more damage, especially if it is a complicated fracture; send for help.

Types of fracture

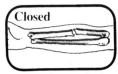

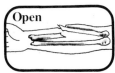

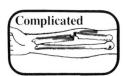

The bone has cracked or broken but is not sticking through the skin.

The broken bone is sticking through the skin making an open wound.

The broken bone has pierced a lung, nerve, blood vessels or the guts.

Sprains and dislocations

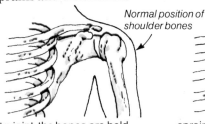

Normal position of shoulder bones

Dislocated shoulder

At a joint, the bones are held together by ligaments. An awkward fall or twist will tear or wrench these ligaments causing a sprain. A wrench may even push a bone right out of place; this is called a dislocation.

Signs of damage

The person will be in pain and may not be able to move his limb. Compare the injured side with the uninjured side. There may be swelling; any discolouration means internal bleeding which could be serious. If a nerve has been damaged there will be numbness and tingling.

What to do

Check to see that the person is breathing (pages 8/9). Do not move the injured part even if there is a lot of swelling – you could do more damage. Allow the person to keep the limb in a position which he feels to be as comfortable as possible.

If the fracture is open (the bone will be sticking through the skin) and the wound is bleeding badly, squeeze the edges of the wound together. Hold the edges together until bleeding has stopped. Cover

Clean dressing

the wound with a clean dressing as quickly as possible to prevent any infection getting into the fractured bone. Don't bandage the wound. Send for help. Reassure the person, and stay with him.

Watch for signs of shock (pages 12/13). Make the person comfortable but don't give anything to drink. If the injury is on

the lower limb, don't remove footwear. Steady a fractured leg to prevent further injury by padding either side with rolled-up clothes.

Falls

If someone has a fall when you are out, give ABC emergency first aid (page 5) and treat for shock (page 13). Don't move him or give him any drinks. Never try to straighten an injured limb. Send someone for help (page 6).

A bang on the head could mean a fractured skull; paralysis or a tingling sensation could mean that a nerve is trapped or the spine is

injured. Don't move the person. However, if the person is unconscious, you must put him in the recovery position and stay with him.

If the injuries are minor, and you really must move the person because help is not available, you can support an injured arm with a sling (page 22). Use a four-handed seat, or a pick-a-back (page 7) to carry someone with a minor foot injury.

General injuries and ailments

Black eye

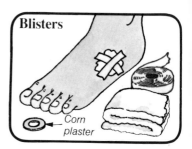

Blisters

Corn plaster

The colour and swelling around a **black eye** is caused by bruising. Reduce the swelling by applying a cold compress or ice bag. Get the patient to a doctor; a blow that has resulted in a black eye may also have caused an eye injury or a skull fracture.

To make a cold compress, soak a cloth in cold water, squeeze out any excess water, and put it on the swelling. As the cloth warms up, soak it again in cold water.

To avoid getting **blisters**, wear well-fitting, comfortable shoes that have been "worn in". If your shoes do begin to rub, cover the sore area with a bandaid or a light, lint dressing held in place by sticking plaster. Ring-shaped corn plasters are useful for taking pressure off the blister. Don't burst the blister. If it has already burst, cut off the flap of skin and, if possible, let it dry out and heal in the open air.

Cramp

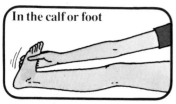

In the calf or foot

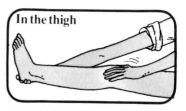

In the thigh

Cramp is caused by a muscle suddenly tightening up. To cure it, rub and stretch the cramping muscle. If it occurs in a calf or foot muscle, straighten the knee and pull the foot towards you. If the cramp is in the thigh, raise the leg with one hand under the heel and

press the knee down with the other hand. Someone who has been sweating a lot after hard exercise may get cramp. Give them one salt tablet or half a teaspoon of salt with a pint of water.

Dirty graze or minor cut (cleaning)

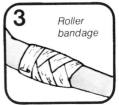
Roller bandage

Wash your hands before you put a dressing on a **cut**. Use lots of fresh water and some clean material to

bathe the cut. Start at the centre and wipe outwards. When the cut and the surrounding skin is free of dirt, dry

thoroughly and put on a bandaid or a clean dressing. If a cut is bleeding badly concentrate on stopping the bleeding.

Earache

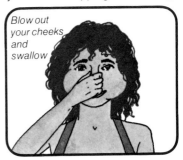
Blow out your cheeks and swallow

The best way to prevent **earache** in cold weather is to keep your ears warm by wearing a hat. If your ears ache after swimming, hold your nose and blow your cheeks

out while swallowing at the same time. If you have persistant earache you may have some sand or an infection in your ear. See a doctor at once.

Ear (an object in the ear) ▶

If you get something in your **ear** (or nose) don't try to get it out – you will end up pushing it further in. Go to a doctor who will remove it for you. If, however, an insect gets into the ear, it can be removed by *gently* flooding the ear with warm water or olive oil. The insect should float out. If you are stung inside the ear, see a doctor at once.

Bottle of olive oil

Electric shock

Don't touch anyone who may have been electrocuted; the electricity can pass through his body and severely injure you. Don't touch anything he is touching. Turn off the switch. Use an object, like a piece of wood, which is not wet, greasy, or made of metal, to push the person away from the source of power, or any wet surfaces. If you can't find a suitable object, pull him away by his clothing, being careful not to touch his flesh. If he has stopped breathing, give artificial respiration (page 9) then treat any burns (pages 14/15). Keep well away from anyone electrocuted by a pylon or a railway line. Go for help.

Eye (something in the eye) ▶

If something gets under the lower lid don't rub your **eye**; look up and pull the lower lid down. Using a damp, soft, clean cloth, gently lift the object out. If something is under the upper lid, look down and pull the upper lid over the lower one; this may dislodge the particle. If the object is on the pupil or is embedded in the eye, see a doctor.

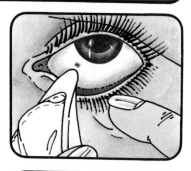

Fainting

Put head between knees

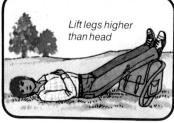

Lift legs higher than head

Fainting occurs when not enough blood reaches the brain; it results in temporary unconsciousness. The cause may be fright, bad news, lack of air or food. There may be some warning beforehand – feeling ill, giddy, or hot and sweaty. Tell the person to sit down; loosen any tight clothing around the neck. Put his head between his knees and tell him to breathe deeply. If, in spite of this, he faints, put his head to one side and lift his legs higher than his head. This will send more blood to the brain and he should recover in a matter of seconds. Slowly raise him into a sitting position. If he doesn't come round, put him in the recovery position (see page 11).

Diabetes

If a diabetic, who has had his morning injection of insulin, becomes pale, sweaty and bad tempered and starts acting in an unreasonable manner, he is about to lose consciousness. Give him two tablespoons of sugar immediately. If he does lose consciousness, he is in danger of dying. Get help immediately.

Headaches

Rest and quiet are the best cures for a **headache**; a short nap or a cup of tea and a meal may also help. Headaches may be a symptom of something else such as stomach trouble. If the headache won't go away, see a doctor.

Hiccups

To get rid of **hiccups**, try holding the breath, breathing deeply or sipping warm water. A fright can sometimes stop hiccups.

Nosebleed ▶

Nosebleeds can be caused by a bad cold or a hit on the nose. Sit down with your head forward so that the blood does not run down your throat. Pinch the nostrils, just below the bony part of the nose, for about 15 minutes. Breathe through the mouth and do not blow your nose for a few hours. If the bleeding won't stop, see a doctor.

Fits

Many healthy people suffer from epileptic **fits.** Fits are not harmful, but they may come on without warning.

With a minor fit the person normally remains standing, but stares straight ahead and does not understand anything said to him. The fit should pass quite quickly. Afterwards, reassure the person, as he may not remember anything.

With a bad fit the person will fall down and become rigid. His arms and legs may jerk about, and he may become red in the face, or froth at the mouth. Don't try to hold him still, but do pull him away by his clothing if he is in a dangerous situation, or is likely to hit something and hurt himself. Be careful that he does not hit or kick you. Move any nearby furniture. When he has stopped jerking about, put a rolled-up hanky between his back teeth and lay him in the recovery position (page 11).

On coming round he will stay confused for some time. Keep an eye on him and, if possible, get him to rest.

Splinters ▶

If the **splinter** is just below the surface of the skin you may be able to remove it with a needle. Sterilize the needle by passing it through the hottest part of a flame. If the splinter is sticking out, try removing it with a pair of tweezers.

Sprays and pesticides ▶

Keep well away from any land which has been sprayed by low-flying aircraft or tractors.

Someone affected by **pesticides** may have a flushed face and shallow breathing. The poison can be absorbed through the skin, so remove the person from the area and take off any clothing covered with spray. Put him in a current of air and sponge his neck and back with cold water. Give sweet drinks.

If breathing stops, give artificial respiration (page 9). Take him to hospital as soon as possible.

Stitch

A **"stitch"** is a sudden pain in the side. It usually occurs after exercise, especially if you are unfit. You may also get a "stitch" if you exercise too soon after eating a meal.

To relieve the pain, try bending over to touch your toes. If this doesn't work, rub the painful part and sip some water. Rest.

Tetanus

Tetanus or "lock jaw" is caused by a bacteria that gets into the body through cuts. If you get a cut when outside, from a garden tool, barbed wire, a rusty nail or an animal bite or scratch, go to a doctor for an anti-tetanus injection.

Toothache

You can ease **toothache** by putting a few drops of oil of cloves on your finger and rubbing the tooth. If the toothache occurs at the weekend when your dentist is closed, look in the phone book to see if there is a dental hospital nearby; they will usually see urgent cases.

Travel sickness

Before you start a long journey, take some pills recommended for **travel sickness**. Take paper bags with you in case of an emergency! When in a car, make sure there is plenty of fresh air, and ask for the car to be stopped if you feel sick. Do not read. Don't eat large meals before or during the journey. Sucking boiled sweets may stop you feeling sick, but don't eat chocolate.

Winding ▶

Winding is caused by a fall, or a blow in the solar plexus (the area just above the stomach). Winding can be very painful and makes breathing difficult. Put the person in the recovery position (page 11) and rub the area above the stomach. Loosen any tight clothing.

Vertigo (giddiness)

Vertigo is severe giddiness caused by fear of heights. If you find yourself with someone who is suffering from vertigo, encourage him to move on. Tell him to breathe deeply and get him to look up or ahead.

If you are on a path near a steep drop, guide the person away from the precipice, and walk between them and the edge.

Making a stretcher

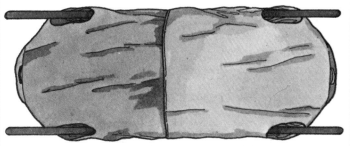

To make a stretcher, turn two coats or jackets the wrong way round, so the sleeves are inside. Button them up and pass two strong poles (tent poles would be ideal) through the sleeves of the coats. Test a home-made stretcher before you carry someone on it.

Never move someone who is seriously injured – you could do more damage.

Signalling for help

Shouting is not the best way to get help, but if someone is injured and you think that there is help nearby, cup your hands round your mouth, and shout something like "Cooee". This sound will travel further than a short cry like "help". Make signals with objects that can be left on show, or signals that can be repeated  at regular intervals; they should have a specific meaning. Don't waste torch batteries or fuel – you may need them later.

Shadow writing

SOS is the best known distress message. Mark SOS out on the ground by piling earth, stones, leaves and clothing into the shape of the letters. The sun or the moon shining on the letters will cast shadows which will outline them. Make each letter as big as possible, about 7-10 metres long, so they will attract a pilot's attention.

Smoke signals

On clear days, attract attention with white smoke. Burn anything damp, like moss, clothes, green branches or leaves.

On dull days, make black smoke by burning rubber, grease or oil; but if fuel is scarce, save it until rescue is in sight.

Three of anything is known internationally as a distress signal. Light three fires in a triangle about 100 paces apart.

Kites and flags

Lay a handkerchief, or a square of material torn from a piece of clothing, on the ground. Try and use a colour that will stand out from the background.

Tie two sticks together in the form of a cross and lay them on the handkerchief. Tie the ends of the sticks to the corners of the handkerchief with some string.

Make a tail with a piece of bandage. Tie a ball of string to the kite at the three points on the sticks as shown.

Write SOS on the cloth, and fly the kite.

If there is no wind, make a flag to wave by attaching a square of cloth to a stick.

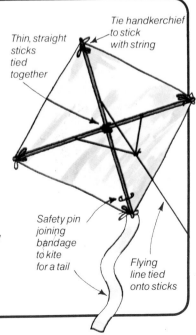

Tie handkerchief to stick with string

Thin, straight sticks tied together

Safety pin joining bandage to kite for a tail

Flying line tied onto sticks

Ground-to-air signals

Directed signals

Use these signals when possible rescue is in sight. Save your torch batteries and fuel for these moments. You can signal directly at the aeroplane or rescue team with a torch or any sort of shiny object: a mirror, a knife blade, a piece of shiny metal, or a tin lid.

> **International mountain distress signal:** six flashes or six whistles per minute.
> Repeat this signal every few minutes. Pause for a minute then repeat. The reply is three flashes per minute, a minute's pause, then three more.

Tin lid

When it is sunny, aim a signal by using a tin lid that is shiny on both sides and has a small hole punched in the middle. Hold it 15 centimetres from your face and look through the hole at the target. Sunlight will form a spot of light on your face which will be reflected on the lid. While looking at the target through the hole, alter the angle of the lid until the light spot disappears. Your target will now receive the flash.

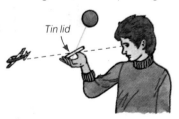

Tin lid

Piece of glass

If the angle between the target and sun is very large, hold the tin lid so a spot of light falls on your hand. Look at the target through the hole and adjust the lid until the reflection of the light spot on your palm disappears.

If you only have a piece of glass, raise the glass in one hand and blot out the target with the other. Reflect the sunlight until it hits your hand. When you lower your hand you will be signalling directly at the aeroplane.

Standard body signals

There are signals that you can use when the rescuer can actually see you. They are all internationally-known signals, recognized by airmen all over the world. By using them you can "speak" to your rescuers. Use your body as a sign, or mark the signs out with stones, clothing or whatever materials are available.

Yes   No

- Don't give up.
- Be prepared for rescue.
- Encourage people with you.
- Keep signalling.

Medical assistance needed urgently

Don't land here   Land here

International ground-to-air signals

Doctor needed

First Aid needed

Unable to go any further

Food and water needed

Yes

No

REMEMBER

WHEN YOU HAVE BEEN RESCUED, CLEAR AWAY YOUR SIGNALS, OTHERWISE SOMEONE MAY WASTE TIME TRYING TO RESCUE YOU AGAIN!!

Heat hazards

In hot and humid climates, the body tries to cool itself by sweating. This results in salt and water loss. Too great a loss of water and salt will result in heatstroke and heat exhaustion. If this occurs, drink a pint of water with half a teaspoon of salt dissolved in it, or take a salt tablet with the water.

Heat exhaustion

The signs are a headache, cramp, feeling sick, clammy and dizzy. Get the person to rest in the shade and give him salt and water.

Heatstroke

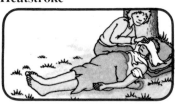

The signs are a high temperature, hot, dry skin and possibly delirium and collapse. Send for help. While you are waiting, get the person's temperature down by fanning him. Wrap him in a wet shirt and put a damp cloth on his face and neck.

Sunburn

The sun can actually burn your skin; a minor burn will be red and itchy, a more serious burn will cause blistering. Water reflects the sun's rays that cause sunburn, so be particularly careful near the sea. Keep your head, neck and shoulders covered, especially at midday when the sun is at its hottest. If you do get burnt, rest in the shade and drink some water. Apply calamine lotion to the red areas. If you have bad blistering, see a doctor.

How to make a water still

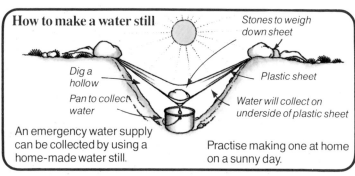

Stones to weigh down sheet

Dig a hollow

Pan to collect water

Plastic sheet

Water will collect on underside of plastic sheet

An emergency water supply can be collected by using a home-made water still.

Practise making one at home on a sunny day.

Sun and snow blindness

Soot or dirt

Card with slits

Band of grass or leaves

Two handkerchiefs knotted together

Handkerchief over face and ears

Hair

Sunglasses

Newspaper hat

The reflection of the sun's rays from snow and water can damage your eyes as well as burn your skin. The pictures above show some of the ways that you can protect your eyes. If you do get sore eyes, cover them with cold compresses (see page 26). As the compresses warm up, wet them again with cold water.

DO'S...

DO SIT IN THE SHADE

DO BOIL WATER FROM PONDS AND STREAMS BEFORE DRINKING IT

DO WEAR LIGHT-COLOURED CLOTHES — THEY REFLECT HEAT

DO KEEP CLOTHES ON — THIS STOPS SWEAT EVAPORATING TOO FAST

DO WIPE FACE, BROW AND BACK OF NECK WITH WATER TO KEEP COOL

DO EAT LITTLE AND OFTEN

... & DON'TS

DON'T WALK IN THE HOTTEST PART OF THE DAY

DON'T DRINK SEA WATER

DON'T WEAR DARK CLOTHES — THEY ABSORB HEAT

DON'T EAT LARGE MEALS — DIGESTING USES A LOT OF WATER

Cold hazards

The effects of exposure to the cold can be very serious, so protect yourself by wearing a hat to keep your head warm, a scarf wrapped round your face, goggles if it is very cold, gloves and warm socks. Eat regularly to give yourself energy and stop and rest if you get tired.

Keeping warm

DO'S · · · ·

DO KEEP MOVING AND JUMP ABOUT

DO BLOW ON FINGERS AND SLAP ARMS ACROSS CHEST

DO MAKE FACES

DO WEAR ALL YOUR CLOTHES. PUT PAPER BAGS OVER HANDS AND FEET.

DO LIGHT A FIRE. A FEW SMALL FIRES WILL BE WARMER THAN ONE BIG ONE

DO EAT HOT FOOD AND DRINK

· · & DON'TS

DON'T SIT ON COLD, WET GROUND. PUT DOWN LEAVES, BRANCHES OR A PLASTIC SHEET FIRST

DON'T GET TOO HOT AND SWEATY — SWEAT CAN FREEZE

Frostbite

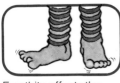
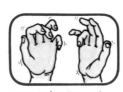

Frostbite affects the parts of the body that are most exposed, such as the fingers, toes, nose, ears and chin. Signs of frostbite are numbness and waxy-looking skin. If you haven't got gloves, put socks on your hands. Wiggle your feet, hands and face to keep the blood flowing. Warm a frost-bitten area slowly; don't try and thaw out in front of a fire.

Exposure

Exposure is caused by continuous chilling from wind, rain and cold. Signs are a general slowing down, blurred speech or eyesight, shivering fits and eventually collapse.

Stop at once and find or make a shelter (ways of sheltering are shown below).

Remove any wet clothes. Put on dry ones. Cover your head, neck and hands.

Get inside a sleeping bag or wrap yourself in a blanket. Cover it with a plastic sheet or spare clothes.

All huddle together. Two people may be able to get into one sleeping bag for extra warmth.

Drink something hot and eat energy-giving foods such as sugar, chocolate, glucose sweets, nuts and dates.

Shelters

Stretch a plastic sheet against a stone wall or boulder. Put something on the ground to sit on and get into your sleeping bag.

Put on extra clothes. Take your arms out of your jacket sleeves and warm them in your armpits. Put your feet in your rucksack.

Shelter behind a boulder. Hug your knees to keep warm.

Make a hollow beside a fallen tree. Use dead branches for a roof.

Make a circle of stones and rocks and huddle together.

Fires in forest and grassland

Fire can be terrifying when out of control. It can spread very fast, sometimes faster than you can run, especially if there is a strong wind. Notice in which direction the fire is spreading. Don't run blindly through the flames. Look for a path, or head for open ground. Cover your face and as much of your body as possible with clothes and blankets. Stay together and keep your face as near to the ground as possible, where the air is most fresh.

Fires at camp

If you can't get hold of water to put out a small fire, smother the flames by shovelling sand or soil over them. You can also beat out the flames with branches or coats.

Trapped in a car

If the fire is on either side of the road, stay in the car and tell the driver to drive fast until you are out of the danger area. Keep all the windows and air vents tightly closed. If the flames are completely surrounding the car, you must still try to drive out of danger. If the car is stationary, the metal body will heat up and the car will act like an oven.

1 Escaping from fire

Try and reach any nearby water and, if you can swim, leap in and wait until the fire has passed. Don't try to outrun the fire, as you will probably be overcome by the heat.

2

If there is no water nearby, scrape a small hollow behind a log or large boulder and lie face down as flat as possible. Cover as much of your body as you can with clothing, blankets or earth.

3

If you are in front of the fire, and you can see a wide path where there are few flames, cover as much of your body as possible, take a deep breath and run through the area as fast as you can.

Clothes on fire

If your clothes catch fire, wrap yourself in the nearest material to hand eg. a coat, blanket or ground-sheet. Leaving your head sticking out, roll over and over on the ground. If someone else is on fire, first pull them to the ground, then wrap them in the nearest available material. If you have wrapped them in something synthetic and it has melted, don't try to remove the material after the flames have been put out – you may pull away burnt skin (pages 14/15).

Natural disasters

Most types of weather conditions will be forecast in advance, so always listen to the local radio before going out. If you do get caught in bad weather, don't struggle on getting cold, wet and tired. Look for shelter.

Lightning

Lightning is attracted to metal such as wire fences, and to solitary boulders, single trees and water. Keep well away from anything standing on its own.

Seek shelter in a wood (avoid the tallest trees), or in the middle of a flat field. Either crouch on the ground, lie on your air mattress or cover yourself with a groundsheet. Make sure that you are not near anything metal, such as a rucksack frame. If someone is hit by lightning and survives, they will have very bad burns (see pages 14/15 and 12/13).

High winds

In strong winds, never walk on narrow mountain ledges or peaks: you could get blown off by a gust. If it suddenly becomes windy, tuck your clothes into your trousers; a flapping coat or jacket can catch the wind and throw you off balance. If the wind is very strong, lie flat on the ground.

Fog, rain and sleet

When you set out walking, you should always carry emergency rations, a waterproof and a spare jumper in case the weather turns bad and you have to stop and shelter. In hilly country, mist can appear very suddenly. You must stop and shelter. It is easy to get lost and you may walk over the edge of a rock face. Stay together.

Floods

Try to avoid camping close to a river. There is a possibility of heavy rain occurring up river and flood water could come rushing down when you are asleep or away from the tent. If there is a flood warning, take food, drinking water and spare clothes, and make for high ground. If you are swept away by flood water, try to grab hold of a floating object such as a log or a piece of wood. If it is big enough, climb on top and use it as a raft. Paddle to safety, using your hands or a piece of wood.

Quicksand and bog

Watch out for quicksands in river beds, especially tidal estuaries and sandy beaches, and for bogs or moors. Clumps of reeds and grasses growing far apart may be a sign of boggy ground.

Throw yourself flat; you will only sink deeper if you struggle. Take off your rucksack and try to put it underneath you. Roll and twist until your feet are free, then "swim" across the bog.

Blizzards

If you are caught in a heavy blizzard, try and find shelter where you can rest instead of struggling on getting cold and tired. If you can't see a hut or shed nearby, you can make a natural shelter from drifts around trees and boulders.

Tree shelter

Plastic sheet

Don't lean against the sides

Boughs and snow on top

Floor of boughs and bark

Scoop out a hole at the side of a tree or boulder and build up a rim around the hole with the snow you dig out. Spread a plastic sheet across it to make a roof; hold it down with snow. Cover the roof with branches or more snow to keep in warmth. Lay a plastic sheet, branches, or bark over the "floor" of the hole.

Earthquakes

If you are in a building when earthquake tremors start, don't run out into the street. Wait in a doorway where you can shelter from falling rubble. If you are in the street, crouch down in the middle of the road with your arms over your head.

Tornadoes

Tornadoes are whirling, funnel-shaped wind storms which suck up everything in their path. Lie flat on the ground, if possible in a cave or hole in the ground. In a building stay away from windows; try to get down to the cellar or basement.

Avalanches

Avalanches are extremely dangerous and can happen very suddenly; they are especially likely to occur during a thaw and after a new fall of snow. Listen to the weather forecasts for your area; if there are any warnings of avalanches don't go out walking or skiing.

Get rid of your skis, ski sticks, ice axes, etc. Try and grab hold of a tree or a rock and hang on. Keep your head down.

If you are swept down with the snow, "swim" with it, trying to keep your head above the surface. Keep your mouth shut.

As the avalanche stops, make a final effort to get to the surface. If you are buried, scoop a hole around your face before the snow freezes. Find out which way up you are by spitting; if the spit lands on your face, you are lying on your back.

REMEMBER
WHEN YOU ARE SKIING OR WALKING ALWAYS STICK TO SKI RUNS OR PATHS. GO IN A GROUP OF AT LEAST THREE.

Danger on water

Accidents can easily happen because people do not take proper care near water. Before you go near any open water, you must be able to swim. Learn in a pool where the shallow and deep ends are marked and there are no currents to swim against. If you are not a strong swimmer, don't go out of your depth.

Find out where it is safe to swim. Beaches with lifeguards fly a red and yellow flag when it is safe, a red one when it is not safe.

Don't swim around sluices, bridges, piers, wrecks or in strong tides, where there will be currents to swim against.

Never dive into water unless it is at least two metres deep, and you can see that the bottom is clear of any rocks or objects.

Don't clamber about on rocks with bare feet. Rocks, shells and sea urchins can cut your feet. Always wear non-slip shoes.

Never play with or lie on an air bed on open water unless it is tied to something on the shore. You could be swept out to sea.

Don't swim straight after a meal, or when you are hungry. Wait for two hours after you have eaten.

Don't stay too long swimming in the water. You can get cold and tired and are therefore more likely to get cramp (page 26).

In open water, swim along the shore rather than out to sea. If you go out too far you may find it difficult to get back.

Don't wade out to sandbanks or around rocky headlands, and don't explore caves. You may get cut off by the tide.

Don't mess around in the water, duck other people or pretend to drown. Don't take any "dares" like swimming out to distant points.

Boats

> IF YOU CAPSIZE KICK OFF HEAVY BOOTS AND TAKE OFF ANY OUTER CLOTHING

Before you take a boat out, find out about the local currents and the times of the tides. Only go out in fine weather, and tell someone where you are going. Don't go out alone. Always wear a life-jacket and take some warm, waterproof clothes and some food with you.

DON'TS

DON'T OVERLOAD A BOAT

DON'T STAND UP OR CHANGE PLACES

DON'T WEAR WELLINGTONS

DON'T GO NEAR OTHER BOATS, ROCKS OR WEIRS

Saving others from water

Only someone experienced in life-saving should swim out to rescue a drowning person. Drowning people panic, and may clutch at the rescuer causing both to drown. So act quickly, go and get help or use one of these methods of rescue.

Victim near bank

Lie flat and hold onto something secure on the bank. Grab the person's wrist (don't let them grab you), or hold out something for them to grab. Let go if you are being dragged into the water.

Victim further out

If the victim is quite far out, throw a rope or anything that floats – a life-belt, swimming ring, beach ball, plank of wood. Don't aim it directly at him; throw it within easy reach!

An object with a line attached is best so you can pull the victim ashore. Hold the line up as you pull him in, to lift him slightly out of the water.

Victim quite far out in shallow water

Make a human chain. The person nearest the shore holds onto something secure, while the others grasp wrists, facing in opposite directions, until someone can reach the victim or throw them a floating object. If you are alone, wade in and try to get near enough to get hold of the victim or to throw him something. Lean backwards and get a firm foothold before you grab hold of him.

Victim a long way out

ONLY ATTEMPT THIS IF YOU CAN ROW WELL

Stern

If, and *only* if, you know how to row well and can handle the type of boat available, row out to the rescue. Approach stern first with the bow facing head on to any current. This is important because the person could capsize you by grabbing the side of the boat. Tell him to hold on to the stern and, if you have a rope, put it under his armpits and tie him to the boat. Tow him ashore, making sure his face is clear of the water. Don't try to get him aboard because you may capsize the boat. If you haven't got a rope, wait with him until help arrives.

Lifebelt

ONLY ATTEMPT THIS IF YOU ARE A GOOD SWIMMER

If no boat is available, and if, and *only* if, you are a very good swimmer, you can swim out to the rescue with a floating object. Make sure first that you can manage the distance; take off bulky clothes and shoes. Although time is important, don't swim so fast that you get tired – remember that you've got to swim back again. Push the floating object towards the person so that he grabs the object rather than you; stay well clear of him. You can then wait until help arrives, return alone to get help, or swim back with him.

49

Saving yourself from water

If you capsize **1**

Inflate your life jacket. Stay with the boat so you can use it to hang on to, and so you will be seen more easily by rescuers.

2

Hang on to the oars or paddles if you can, but don't risk losing the boat; it could get swept away by wind or currents.

3

Tie yourself to the boat, so that you won't lose it if you get tired and lose your grasp.

4

Signal by holding up an oar with a piece of brightly coloured clothing tied to it.

5

If there is a storm and it is difficult to hold on to the boat, swim underneath and hang on to the seats until the weather improves.

Floating

If you lose the boat and are getting tired, relax by floating. Keep your chin and face out of the water.

Save warmth and energy

REMEMBER,
ALWAYS WEAR
YOUR LIFE
JACKET

Keep on one layer of clothing to retain some heat. Save energy and stay warm by holding your arms tight against your sides with your knees raised. If there are several of you, keep your arms around each other.

How to make a lifebelt

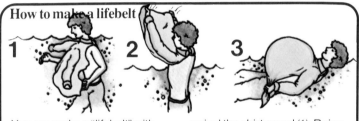

You can make a "lifebelt" with trousers, but a shirt is easier, since you lose less energy taking it off. Take your arms out of the sleeves; do up the top two buttons, and swivel the shirt round (1). Raise the bottom of the shirt (2). Bring the shirt down quickly so air is trapped under it (3). As the air leaks out, trap some more.

How to get into a lifebelt

This is not as easy as it looks, so practise a few times in the local baths. Push the side nearest to you underwater, so that the other side sticks up. Push the bottom edge away from you so that the belt begins to fall over your head. As it drops over your head, raise one arm and put it through, then put the other arm through.

51

Landing on rocks

If you have to land on rocks, aim for a point where the waves are calmest. Ride in on a wave with your feet forward to act as a buffer.

Lurch forward, try and get a hand-hold, then scramble on to the rocks as quickly as possible before you are pulled off by the sea.

If trapped by an incoming tide ...

Don't attempt to climb a cliff face if it has no footholds or is too high.

Don't climb a cliff face which looks crumbly, or which might have loose rocks further up.

Look for a secure ledge above the high tide mark, and wait until the tide goes out again.

If your shoes are slippery, take them off; either climb in socks, or put socks over your shoes.

REMEMBER

IF YOU ARE GOING FOR A WALK ON THE BEACH, ALWAYS CHECK THE TIMES OF TIDES SO THAT YOU DON'T GET CUT OFF

Points to remember

Whatever you are doing – walking, cycling or sailing, always go out in a group of at least three. If you are going rowing or sailing, always wear a life jacket.

Before you go out, check the weather forecast in the paper or on radio or television in case bad weather is on the way.

Work out a plan of your route; leave a copy with someone saying where you are going and what time you expect to be back.

Some camp sites have message boxes which are checked. Leave your route and expected return time there.

REMEMBER
REMOVE MESSAGES
ON YOUR RETURN,
OTHERWISE A
SEARCH PARTY
MIGHT BE SENT OUT
TO LOOK FOR YOU

When out and about

DO GO OUT IN A PARTY OF AT LEAST THREE

DO TAKE MAP, COMPASS AND EXTRA CLOTHES

DO LOOK FOR SHELTER IF THE WEATHER BECOMES STORMY

DON'T WALK AFTER DARK. IF YOU HAVE TO, FACE ONCOMING TRAFFIC AND USE YOUR TORCH

NEVER HITCH-HIKE ALONE, EVEN IN EMERGENCIES

Poisonous plants

Never eat any berries, nuts, seeds, roots, leaves, or flowers on a plant unless you definitely know that they are edible. Don't think that the plant is edible just because an animal has been eating it; the animal may not be affected by the poisons. Avoid red berries – they are usually poisonous. Don't eat any mushrooms or toadstools in the wild – it is easy to confuse poisonous and edible ones.

Plants poisonous to the touch

Poison Ivy

Poison Sumac

Poison Oak

The plants shown above are all found in North America, and are poisonous to the touch. They will bring you out in a rash or blisters.

If you touch one, wash with soap and water. The poisons can be carried in smoke, so don't burn the wood of these plants.

Deadly poisonous plants

Red

Holly
*Poisonous berries,
Symptoms: very bad
sickness.*

Red

Yew
*Poisonous leaves,
berries. Symptoms:
sickness, diarrhoea,
clammy skin, trembling.*

Black

Deadly Nightshade
*Poisonous berries.
Symptoms: high
temperature, great thirst.*

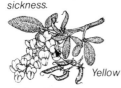

Yellow

Laburnum
*All parts are poisonous.
Symptoms: burning in
mouth and throat,
headache, stomach-
ache.*

White

Hemlock
*All parts are poisonous.
Sore throat, muscular
weakness, trembling,
sickness.*

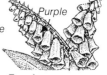

Purple

Foxglove
*All parts are poisonous.
Symptoms: stomach-
ache, headache,
sickness, dizziness,
drowsiness.*

Deadly poisonous fungi

Colour varies from dirty white to green

Cap is yellowish grey

Red cap with white warts

Gills, ring and stalk are white

Gills, stalk and ring are white

Bulbous sheath

Gills at first yellowish, later go pinkish with age

Fly Agaric
Symptoms appear half an hour to four hours later: sickness, giddiness, visions.

Death Cap
Symptoms appear many hours later: sickness, great pain, diarrhoea, collapse, coma.

Livid Entoloma
Symptoms appear soon: sickness, weakness, diarrhoea, pain.

Food poisoning and its three main symptoms

You can get food poisoning from eating bad food. Avoid stale food, or food that smells "off". Canned food can also go off; if a can is badly dented or punctured, or bulges at one end, throw it away.

1

Pain and cramp around the stomach

2

Diarrhoea; feeling sick.

3

Possible headache; blurred vision, dizziness; weakness.

<u>WHAT TO DO IF SOMEONE IS POISONED</u>

1. PHONE FOR AN AMBULANCE.
2. IF NO HELP IS AT HAND, YOU COULD TRY TO MAKE YOURSELF SICK BY STICKING YOUR FINGERS DOWN YOUR THROAT.
3. PUT AN UNCONSCIOUS PERSON IN THE RECOVERY POSITION.
4. TAKE SOME OF THE BERRIES OR LEAVES THAT HAVE CAUSED THE POISONING TO THE HOSPITAL WITH YOU.

Animals that sting

Bees, hornets and wasps

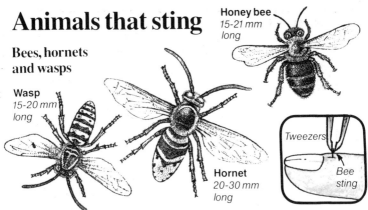

Honey bee
15-21 mm
long

Wasp
15-20 mm
long

Hornet
20-30 mm
long

Tweezers

Bee sting

Bees, wasps and hornets will normally leave you alone as long as you leave them alone, so don't rush around trying to swat them: they may get angry and sting you. Keep calm and wait until they fly off. Bees sting only once and then die; wasps and hornets can sting more than once. Bees leave their sting in the flesh; get it out quickly with your fingernails, a pair of tweezers or a sterilized needle. Don't squeeze a sting – you will push the poison further into the flesh. Don't scratch it – this will make it itch more. The irritation usually wears off after an hour or so.

Stings in the mouth

Watch out for wasps and bees when eating sweet food. If someone is stung in the mouth or throat, call a doctor. While waiting for help get them to wash their mouth with a solution of bicarbonate of soda (one teaspoonful in a glass of water). If breathing is difficult, put them in the recovery position (page 11).

Bee swarms

If you find yourself next to a disturbed nest, stay still for a few minutes until the bees have calmed down, then move slowly away. About once a year bees look for a new nest site; they leave the old nest in a great swarm. Don't panic if a swarm comes near you; they are not attacking and will ignore you.

Removing ticks

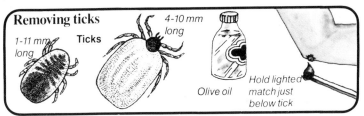

Ticks

1-11 mm long

4-10 mm long

Olive oil

Hold lighted match just below tick

Ticks feed on blood. They bury their mouthparts into the skin and cling on firmly while feeding. If you are camping, keep a watch for ticks on your skin, as they can pass on diseases. They are difficult to pull out as their body often breaks off leaving the head embedded. You can get them to drop off by holding a lighted match near them, but you may also burn yourself. The best way to remove a tick is to coat it with oil. Leave the oil on for a while and then pull the tick out with a pair of tweezers.

Mosquitoes

Mosquito bites give you itchy lumps; these will keep itching for several days and can be very irritating when you get hot. Mosquitoes are not dangerous, but in the tropics they can pass on malaria. Use an insect-repelling cream and keep as much of your skin covered as possible. Camp on high ground away from swampish water where mosquitoes breed. They are attracted to body heat and sweat, so even though you may be feeling hot, keep you clothes on at night to protect your skin.

Treating insect bites

Soap

Calamine lotion

Bicarbonate of soda

Don't scratch an insect bite. This will only make it itch more, and dirt under your finger nails may get into the bite and cause an infection. To keep the swelling down, apply a paste of bicarbonate of soda (use spit if you have no water); calamine lotion may reduce the itching. If you have nothing else, soap or even mud spread over the bite will help.

Dangerous animals

Snakes

Leave snakes alone – don't try to kill them. They will want to escape rather than attack, and will bite only in order to defend themselves.

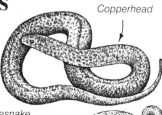

Copperhead

Rattlesnake

Common Brown Snake

Taipan

Adder

THIS WARNING APPLIES TO ANY POISONOUS BITE

GET THE PERSON TO HOSPITAL AS SOON AS POSSIBLE. TRY TO REMEMBER WHAT THE ANIMAL LOOKED LIKE SO THAT THE HOSPITAL WILL KNOW WHAT ANTI-VENOM TO GIVE. KEEP THE PERSON CALM. GET HIM TO LIE DOWN. WASH THE BITE WITH SOAP AND WATER IF POSSIBLE. SUPPORT AND IMMOBILIZE THE LIMB. GET MEDICAL HELP IMMEDIATELY. IF BREATHING STOPS, GIVE ARTIFICIAL RESPIRATION (SEE PAGE 9)

DO'S.... ...& DON'TS

DO WEAR THICK SOCKS AND STRONG SHOES

DO WALK NOISILY. SNAKES ARE TIMID CREATURES AND DON'T WANT TO MEET YOU

DON'T PUT YOUR HANDS IN HOLES OR CREVICES. MAKE SURE YOU LOOK WHERE YOU PUT THEM

Jellyfish

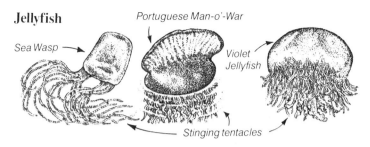

Portuguese Man-o'-War

Sea Wasp →

Violet Jellyfish

Stinging tentacles

The jellyfish shown above can give you very nasty stings that can be fatal. Most jellyfish stings, however, are not dangerous; they can be treated by pouring methylated spirits or alcohol over the area. Calamine lotion will ease the pain. If you do come across small jellyfish when swimming, splash them out of the way.

Spiders and scorpions

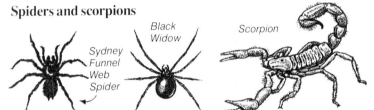

Sydney Funnel Web Spider

Black Widow

Scorpion

Britain has no scorpions and no poisonous spiders. However, there are poisonous species in warmer parts of the world. Scorpions usually live in rocky areas and in stone walls. Spiders can be found under rocks, logs, in holes and crevices and sometimes in houses.

DO'S ....& DON'TS

DO CHECK YOUR BED BEFORE GETTING IN

DO WEAR SHOES WHEN YOU ARE OUTSIDE

DO CHECK YOUR CLOTHES AND SHOES BEFORE DRESSING

DO CHECK YOUR CAMP SITE. TURN OVER STONES WITH A STICK

DON'T MOVE LOGS, ROCKS OR STONES WITH BARE HANDS

Dangerous animals

Very few animals are aggressive. Most wild animals will run away rather than attack, unless they are cornered and cannot escape. Even pets can become dangerous if frightened or roughly handled. If you treat animals with respect and keep your distance, they should ignore you.

In the mating season

Animals may become dangerous during their mating season. Male deer, normally shy, become very aggressive in the autumn, when they begin mating.

Animals with young

All animals can be dangerous when they are protecting their young. Don't approach any baby animal: its mother will be nearby and may attack you.

Charging animals

If by accident, you find yourself in a field with a bull, don't panic. Keep watching the animal and walk calmly towards the nearest fence. If it charges, run as fast as you can, dropping whatever you are carrying and throwing off any

easily removable pieces of clothing. This may distract the animal, giving you valuable seconds to escape. Bulls don't like water, so a river or lake is a good escape route from them.

Dogs

Dogs are usually friendly, but occasionally you will meet a dog that is nervous or bad-tempered. Try not to show that you are frightened, and back away slowly. Keep clear of any strange dogs you meet outdoors, especially fighting dogs or packs of dogs.

DO'S & DON'TS

DON'T PAT A STRANGE DOG – IT MAY NOT LIKE BEING TOUCHED AND MIGHT BE AFRAID OF STRANGERS

DON'T SHOW THAT YOU ARE FRIGHTENED_ A DOG CAN SENSE THIS AND MAY BECOME BOLDER

DON'T TURN YOUR BACK AND RUN AWAY_ THE DOG WILL ONLY CHASE AFTER YOU. BACK AWAY SLOWLY

IF YOU ARE RIDING A BICYCLE AND A DOG STARTS TO CHASE YOU . . . .

DO GET OFF AND WALK, KEEPING THE BICYCLE BETWEEN YOU AND THE DOG

DON'T TRY TO RACE AWAY FROM THE DOG– IT WILL FOLLOW AND MAY CAUSE AN ACCIDENT

Rabies

Rabies is a very dangerous disease that has no cure once symptoms show. Any warm-blooded animal can be infected after being bitten by a rabies-infected animal. In Europe, foxes are the most common victims, but domestic animals such as dogs, cats and cattle also catch rabies.

When you are in countries where rabies occurs, keep well away from stray dogs and cats even if they appear docile. Mostly, a rabid dog will appear withdrawn, and not show any obvious symptoms. But a rabid dog may become very aggressive and attack without warning; cats may also attack and bite. Don't touch any dead animals.

If you are bitten by any dog in a country where rabies occurs, first wash the bite thoroughly with soap and water (detergent actually kills the rabies virus). Then see a doctor as soon as possible. Try to remember what the dog looked like and where the incident occurred so the animal can be caught and examined. Rabies does not occur in Britain at the present time.

Book list

First Aid Manual. The authorized manual of the British Red Cross Society, St John Ambulance and St Andrew's Ambulance Association.
The British Red Cross Society Practical First Aid Manual (E.P. Publishing.)
The Essentials of First Aid. An authorized manual of St John Ambulance.

Modern First Aid. A.S. Playfair (Hamlyn).
First Aid for Hill Walkers and Climbers. Jane Renout and Stewart Hulse (Penguin).
Life Saving and Water Safety. (The Royal Life Saving Society.)
The Spur Book of Survival and Rescue. Terry Brown and Rob Hunter (Spur).

Useful addresses

British Red Cross Society
9 Grosvenor Crescent,
London SW1.
Runs an eight-session **Accident Prevention Course** suitable for all age groups, covering many aspects including water safety, road safety (for pedestrians and cyclists), and home accidents. Also runs an **Emergency First Aid Course,** a practical course in two to four sessions, covering the life-saving procedures and principles of First Aid.
St John Ambulance Association, 29 Weymouth Street, London W1. Write for information about talks in schools.

Royal Life Saving Society
Desborough House,
14 Devonshire Street, Portland Place, London W1. The society runs courses in life saving and water safety at local branches.

The organizations listed above also arrange for talks to be given in schools. If you are at school and would be interested to have any of these talks, ask your teacher if this might be arranged. The addresses of headquarters are given above. To find out about local branches of any of these organizations, ask at your local library.

Index

accidents, 5-7; on water, 46-7
ailments, general, 26-31; see also
    under individual ailments
ambulance service, 6
animals, 56-61; dangerous, 60-1;
    poisonous, 58-9
artificial respiration, 8-9

bandages, 18-23; crepe, 21; in an
    emergency kit, 4, 5; how to
    fasten, 19; types of, 18-19
bandaging, 20-3
bites, insect, 57; mosquito, 57;
    snake, 58
bleeding, 5, 16-17, 20-1; internal, 17;
    see also blood; nosebleed
blisters, on feet, 26; from
    poisonous plants, 54
blizzards, 44; see also weather
blood, 17; circulation, 12; loss of,
    16; see also bleeding
breathing, 5, 8-9; in an
    unconscious person, 10-11
bruising, 17, 25
burns, 14-15; bandaging, 20, 23;
    chemical, 14; from electricity, 14;
    from lightning, 42

choking, 8
clothing, removing from burns, 14;
    what to do if it catches fire, 41;
    to keep warm, 39, 43;
    waterproof, 43
cold, hazards, 38-9; protection
    from, 38, 51
coma, as symptom of poisoning,
    55; see also unconsciousness
compress, cold, 26
consciousness, 5, 10-11
corn plasters, 26
cramp, in limbs, 26; stomach, 55
cuts, 20-1, 23; cleaning, 27

diabetes, 29
diarrhoea, as symptom of
    poisoning, 54, 55
dislocations, 24-5
dizziness, 54, 55
dressing, pad, 16; sterile, 18;
    see also bandages
drowsiness, 10, 54

earache, 27
ears, objects in, 27
electric shock, 28
emergency, call (making a), 6; kit,
    4-5; rations, 5, 39; services, 6
exposure, 39
eyes, black, 26; blindness, caused
    by sun or snow, 37; object in,
    28; protection from sun, 37;
    see also vision

fainting, 28
fire, and clothing, 41; at camp, 40;
    in forest and grassland, 40-1;
    prevention in road accidents, 7;
    see also burns
fits, 29
flags, for signalling, 33
floods, 43
food, high-energy, 5, 39
fractures, 24-5
frostbite, 38
fungi, deadly poisonous, 55

giddiness, as symptom of
    poisoning, 54; see also vertigo

headaches, 29, 54, 55
heart, what to do if it stops, 9
heat hazards, 36-7
heatstroke, 36
heat exhaustion, 36
hiccups, 29

injuries, carrying someone with, 7; general, 26-31; slings for arm and shoulder, 22
internal bleeding, 17

life-belt, 48, 49; how to get into, 51; how to make a, 51
life-jacket, 47, 51
ligaments, 24
lightning, how to avoid, 44
lock jaw, see tetanus

malaria, 57
mouth, burning in, 54

narrow bandage, 18, 19; how to make a, 19; see also bandages
natural disasters, 42-5
nosebleed, 29

pesticides, 30
plants, poisonous, 54-5
plasma, 14, 15
poisoning, food, 55; from pesticides, 30; from plants, 54-5; from snakes, 58; symptoms of, 54-5
pressure pad, 16
pulse, how to take a, 12-13; rate, 13

rabies, 61
rash, from plants, 54
recovery position, 11
reef knot (for tying bandages), 19
rescue, signalling for, 32-5; from water, 48-9
ring pad, 18-19; how to make a, 19
roller bandage, 18; using a, 16, 20-1, 27; see also bandages

safety, in bad weather, 42-3; in boats, 47; hints, 53; in the sun, 37, 56; water, 46-7
salt, 26, 36; tablets, 26, 36

shelter, from cold, 39; from earthquakes, 44; from lightning, 42; tree, 44
shock, 12-13, 14, 17, 25; how to treat, 13; see also electric shock
signals, for help, 32-5
slings, 22
snakes, poisonous, 58; bites, 58
snow blindness, see eyes
splinters, 30
sprains, 24
stings, 56-7; bee, 56; hornet, 56; jellyfish, 59; wasp, 56
stitch (pain in the side), 30
stomach-ache, from food poisoning, 55; from poisonous plants, 54
stretcher, making a, 31
stupor, 10
suffocation, 8
sun blindness, see eyes
sunburn, 36

tetanus, 30
throat, burning in, 54; sore (as symptom of poisoning), 54
toothache, 30
tourniquet, 16
travel sickness, 31
triangular bandage, 5, 18-19, 22-3

unconsciousness, 10-11

vertigo, 31
vision, blurred, 55
visions, 55

water, danger in, 46-7; loss of from the body, 36
water still, how to make a, 36
weather, forecasts, 42, 53; hazardous, 42-4
winding, 31
wounds, see cuts; bandaging